What Jesus Taught

Hubert Richards

THE LITURGICAL PRESS
Collegeville, Minnesota

McCrimmons
Great Wakering, Essex

First published 1992 by McCrimmon Publishing Co Ltd,
10-12 High Street, Great Wakering, Essex SS3 0EQ
Telephone 0702 218956; Fax 0702 216082

McCrimmons   ISBN 0 85597 482 6
The Liturgical Press ISBN 0-8146-2197-X

Cover design by Paul Shuttleworth
Typesetting & layout by McCrimmon Publishing Co Ltd.
Printed by Black Bear Press, Cambridge

INTRODUCTION

Jesus taught many things.
Read the Gospel ('The Good News') to see how his friends
remembered the good things he taught.

But of all the good things Jesus taught, three stand out:

> The words he taught his friends to say when they
> turned to God in prayer. These words are known
> as **The Lord's Prayer.**

> The list of people he pointed to as the really lucky ones.
> This list is known as **The Beatitudes**.

> The stories he told to show people how God is
> surprisingly different from what they imagine.
> These stories are known as **The Parables.**

This book tries to help you understand these things taught
by Jesus.

THE LORD'S PRAYER

Praying to God is difficult.
He is so close to us, yet so far away.
We wouldn't know *how* to pray, or how to do it *properly*,
    unless someone taught us.
There are right ways of praying, and wrong ways.

The first friends of Jesus knew how close he was to God.
So they asked him to teach them how to speak to God.
He taught them **The Lord's Prayer.**
They have taught it to us.
We can pray 'with confidence
    in the words our Saviour gave us.'

We feel safe with a good father or mother

OUR FATHER

One of the words we use to speak about God is 'Father'.
We turn to God as easily as we turn to a good father.
We speak to God as freely as we speak to a loving
    mother.

Jesus was very fond of this word 'Father'.
He was Jewish, and this is one of the words the Jews
    have always used for God.
We feel safe with a good father or mother.
They brought us into the world, and cared for us day
    after day.
They fed us, and taught us, and protected us.
They helped us become adults.

> *I turn to you, God, as easily as I would turn to my*
> *   own parents.*
> *You are my father, just as you are the father of all*
> *   my brothers and sisters across the world.*
> *Our Father!*

The sky takes my breath away

WHO ART IN HEAVEN

God is like a parent.
But he is also completely different from all the parents I
    know.
He is a 'Father in Heaven'.

'Heaven' is a word we use to speak
    of something completely above us,
    something completely beyond our grasp.
Heavens above! Good Heavens! Heaven knows!
God is mysterious.

> *You are as close to us, God, as any parent can be.*
> *But you are also as far above us as the sky.*
> *When I look at the sky, it takes my breath away.*
> *God my Father, I feel you so close.*
> *God in Heaven, how can I be close to you?*

HALLOWED BE THY NAME

Jesus's heart is full of wonder before God.
The first thing he says to him is what all Jews say:
    'Hallowed be thy name', or
    'Hallelujah', or
    'Blessed be God.'

> *Glory to God in the highest.*
> *We worship you.*
> *We give you thanks.*
> *We praise you for your glory.*

God rules O.K.

THY KINGDOM COME

We call God our Father.
We also call him our King.
We belong to God not only in the way we belong to our parents.
We belong to God in the way people belong to a king.

When we pray for God's Kingdom to come,
    we long for the day we can say, 'God rules O.K.'
Jesus added the warning:
    'The Kingdom of God is in *your* hands.

> **God our King,**
>   **the kingdom comes**
>   **when people are fair to each other,**
>   **the Kingdom comes**
>   **when people care for each other,**
>   **the Kingdom comes**
>   **when people forgive each other.**
> **Thy Kingdom come!**

THY WILL BE DONE ON EARTH
AS IT IS IN HEAVEN

God's Kingdom will come when his great plan is carried
    out as perfectly in the world as it is in heaven.
Jesus said that this world could be a heaven on earth.
But that won't come about easily.

In the world as it is, it can be painful to carry out God's plan.
Even Jesus shrank back when he had to face suffering.
But he still said, 'Thy will be done.'

> **Father in heaven,**
>   **we long for our world to be as you planned it,**
>   **even if we have to suffer to make it so.**
> **Thy will be done.**

N. C. C.
TRESPASSERS
WILL BE
PROSECUTED

John Fisher

Jesus says trespassers will be forgiven

GIVE US THIS DAY OUR DAILY BREAD

We need food to live.
Every day.
Those who don't have food starve and die.
We must ask God every day to *give* us our food,
    so that we always remember *he* provides it.

> **God our Father,**
>   **we are like children sitting at your full table,**
>   **who know how to say 'please'.**
> **You have provided a world**
>   **where there is enough food to feed everyone.**
> **Help us to see that everyone gets a fair share.**

FORGIVE US OUR TRESPASSES

We don't only need bread.
We need, again and again, to be forgiven
    for all the wrong things we do.
The notice in the field says, 'Trespassers will *not* be
    forgiven.'
Jesus says our sins *will* be forgiven.
We have only to ask.

> **God our Father, we are not afraid to tell you**
>   **all the wrong things we do.**
> **Jesus has told us you do not hold them against us.**
> **When we ask you to forgive us,**
>   **it is not because we are afraid you won't.**
> **It is because we need to hear,**
>   **over and over again,**
>   **the wonderful news that you do *forgive* us**

A trial of strength

AS WE FORGIVE THOSE
WHO TRESPASS AGAINST US

Peter once asked Jesus how often he ought to forgive
  someone who had done him wrong.
Boasting as usual, he offered to do it seven times.

Jesus said,'That's very generous!
        But God is even more generous!
        Multiply that by seventy,
        and you still won't be like God!
        God goes on and on forgiving.
        And you must do the same.'

> *God our Father,*
>   *we can't call ourselves your children*
>   *if we are not like you, always forgiving.*
> *Like father, like son.*
> *Teach us to be your sons and daughters.*

AND LEAD US NOT INTO TEMPTATION

Temptation means testing, a trial of strength.
If there were to be any testing of our strength,
  we might get a very low score.
We know how weak we are.
And we're not afraid to tell God we are afraid.

> *God our Father,*
> *Jesus told his friends to pray*
>   *that they would not be put to the test.*
> *He knew how weak they were.*
> *We know how weak we are too.*
> *We gladly pray the same.*
> *Do not put us to the test.*
> *We might fail you.*

BUT DELIVER US FROM EVIL

Knowing how weak we are,
  we ask God to rescue us from anything that could
  harm us.
The evil that could harm our body.
And the worse evil that could harm our soul.
The evil that people could do to us.
And the worse evil we could do to ourselves.

God our Father,
All you have ever wanted is to set people free.
You rescued your people Israel from slavery.
And you rescued your Son Jesus from the dead.
Come and rescue us, and make us free.

Come and rescue us

FOR THINE IS THE KINGDOM, AND THE POWER AND THE GLORY, FOR EVER AND EVER

The **Lord's Prayer** began with words that praise God.
To balance them, Christians have added these words of
   praise at the end.
They didn't want to finish the prayer
   pointing to themselves,
   but pointing back to God.
He is the beginning and end of all our prayers.

> *Glory be to the Father,*
> *And to the Son,*
> *And to the holy Spirit of God that makes them one.*

Thine is the glory

AMEN

Jesus finished his prayer with a word
  which comes at the end of many Jewish prayers:
  Amen.
It means   Yes.
          Hear Hear!
          I agree.
          I go along with that.
We ought not to say *Amen* to a prayer
  unless we really mean what it says.

  God our Father,
  when we ask for anything in our prayer to you,
  we say* Amen *with confidence.
  We know that when we ask for bread,
  you would not give us a stone.

I agree with that

IN THE LORD'S PRAYER, THE LORD JESUS HAS TAUGHT US TO SAY:

God of all the people in the world,
close to us as a father or mother,
yet far beyond us as the sky,
we fall on our knees in wonder before you.

We long for your Kingdom,
when all people will live in your way,
and the world will be a heaven on earth.

Unless you give us food every day, we will die:
teach us to share it fairly.
Unless you forgive us every day, we will be without
hope:
teach us to forgive others the way you do.

If you put us to the test,
you know how easily we could let you down.
Rescue us therefore,
as you have always rescued your people.

For you are the God we will always turn to,
in sorrow and in joy.

We mean this.

THE BEATITUDES

The friends of Jesus once asked him:
    'Who are the really happy people?'
What would you have said?
Those who have lots of money and plenty to eat?
Those who are important and can boss others around?
Those who are strong and never get hurt?

Jesus surprised everybody by saying the opposite.
The *really* happy people, he said,
    are the 'nobodies' of this world.
    The poor.
    The unimportant.
    The hungry.
    The heartbroken.
    The peaceful.
    The persecuted.
Why would he say that?

i. Blessed are the poor in spirit,
for theirs is the Kingdom of Heaven.

1. HOW LUCKY YOU ARE
IF YOU ARE POOR!
GOD WILL MAKE YOU RICH!

What a riddle!
Why would anyone call the poor 'lucky'?
Aren't they *unlucky*?
Jesus said no, they are lucky. Why?
Because nothing stands between them and God.
If they want, they can see God more clearly
    than people who are so cluttered with things
    that God is hidden from them.
    The more things people have,
    the less they think about God.
Who, then are the really lucky ones?

Forgive us, Lord,
    for surrounding ourselves
    with so many things
    that we can no longer
    see you.
For everything we have is
    your gift to us, and those
    whose hands are empty
    know that best.

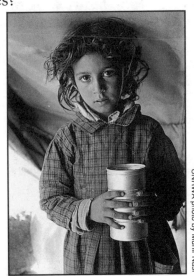

Empty

ii. Blessed are the meek,
for they shall possess the land

2. HOW LUCKY YOU ARE IF YOU'RE NOT VERY IMPORTANT! GOD WILL MAKE YOU GREAT!

The same riddle.
Why would anyone call you lucky if you're unimportant?
Because you're important to God,
    and that's all that matters.
Those who push you around think *they* are God.
What a funny idea of God they have!
The real God is on your side, not theirs.
How lucky you are!

> **Forgive us, Lord,**
>   **for wanting to be more important than others,**
>   **when even the unimportant**
>   **are important to you,**
>   **and that's all that matters.**
> **Help us to see other people the way you see them.**

iii. Blessed are they that mourn,
for they shall be comforted

3. HOW LUCKY YOU ARE
IF YOUR HEART HAS BEEN BROKEN!
IT WILL MEND EVEN STRONGER!

An even stranger puzzle!
Why congratulate people for being in trouble?
Shouldn't we take pity on them?
Of course we should.
But perhaps we should also envy them.
Trouble might have made them stronger than those
    who've always had an easy life.
And trouble might have brought them closer to others
    in trouble.
Only broken hearts can help other broken hearts.

Forgive us, Lord,
    for being so quick to complain
    about our own troubles,
    and so slow to see the
    troubles other people have.
Help us use our troubles to grow
    strong,
    so that we can help others.

UNRWA photo by Munir Nasr

Broken heart

25

iv. Blessed are they that hunger and thirst after justice,
for they shall have their fill

4. HOW LUCKY YOU ARE
IF YOU'RE STARVING.
YOU'LL GET ALL YOU WANT AND MORE!

Why congratulate people for being hungry?
Because when there's food to be eaten,
    it's no good inviting people who are well fed.
Only those who are really hungry will enjoy the food.
So they're the really lucky ones.
Especially if they're hungry to see
    that everyone else gets what is needed.
Because that is what God is hungry for.

> *Thank you, Lord,*
>   *for providing us with so many good things,*
>   *that we never really go hungry,*
>   *and hardly know what it means to be starving.*
> *Open our eyes to the needs of those who haven't got*
>   *what we've got,*
>   *because you have called them the lucky ones.*
> *And give food to the hungry.*

v. Blessed are the merciful,
for they shall obtain mercy

5. HOW LUCKY YOU ARE
IF YOU ARE TENDER WITH OTHERS!
YOU KNOW HOW TENDER GOD REALLY IS!

Many people find it hard to think of God as
   tender, gentle and forgiving.
When they think of the wrong they've done,
   the very thought of God scares them.
Jesus tells them they are mistaken.
There *is* no punishing God.
The real God is as tender as a mother,
   for whom nothing is unforgivable.
And those who are tender with others are lucky,
   because they're becoming just like God.

> **Forgive us, Lord,**
>   **for being hard and unforgiving with others,**
>   **and even with ourselves.**
> **It shows how little we know you as you really are.**
> **Tell us again and again**
>   **the good news that you**
>   **forgive us,**
>   **so that we can grow into**
>   **forgiving people.**

UNRWA photo by George Nehmeh

Tender as a mother

6. HOW LUCKY YOU ARE
IF YOU'RE STRAIGHT WITH PEOPLE!
YOU SEE GOD VERY CLEARLY INDEED!

Some people think that the way to get to the top is to cheat.
But the 'top' you get to that way is nowhere near God.
God is utterly honest and fair.
He is totally truthful and reliable.
He never lets anyone down.
It is only those who are like that who get close to God.
Aren't they lucky!

Straight

Forgive us, Lord,
for so often being crooked
instead of straight,
unfair instead of fair,
cheating instead of honest,
pretending instead of open.
How can we complain that we
can't see you,
when we're the very opposite
of you?

Syndication International

vii. Blessed are the peacemakers,
for they shall be called the children of God.

7. HOW LUCKY YOU ARE
IF YOU MAKE FRIENDS WITH PEOPLE!
YOU'VE BROUGHT A BIT OF HEAVEN TO
EARTH!

It's easy to be friends with people who are just like you.
It's harder with people who are quite different from you.
It's hardest of all with people
    who are so different they hate you.
You feel like hating them back: they're your enemies.
Jesus says, Don't.
That will only spread the misery.
You can't call God your Father unless you love people
    the way he loves them.
That will turn them into friends.

> **Forgive us, Lord,**
> **for often making more enemies than friends.**
> **That way will never turn the world into a paradise,**
> **   only a hell.**
> **Teach us your way of**
> **   spreading friendship**
> **   to everyone,**
> **   and treating them**
> **   as we'd like them**
> **   to treat us.**

Friends

29

A new world

viii. Blessed are they that suffer persecution for justice' sake, for theirs is the Kingdom of Heaven.

8. HOW LUCKY YOU ARE IF PEOPLE HATE YOU FOR STANDING UP FOR WHAT'S RIGHT! A NEW WORLD CAN BE BUILT ON PEOPLE LIKE YOU!

Another riddle to finish with!
Why admire people for being hated?
If they're hated for doing wrong, we wouldn't admire them.
But if they're hated for doing right, we ought to.
Because it's only those who stand up for what is right
    who can make the world into a better place.
How lucky to be one of them!

> *Forgive us, Lord,*
>   *for being such cowards*
>   *in standing up for what is right.*
> *It's much easier to say what other people say,*
>   *and do what they do.*
> *Give us the courage to do what we know is right,*
>   *whatever other people say,*
>   *because that's the only way a new world*
>   *can be built.*

WHO ARE THE REALLY HAPPY PEOPLE?

Those who have met Jesus and seen
 how he took the side of the poor and the unimportant,
 how he pitied those with a broken heart,
 how hungry he was to see right done,
 how gentle he was with everyone,
 how straight and honest he always was,
 how he loved even those
 who hated him enough to kill him,
and have realized that this is exactly what GOD is like.

Those who want to find real happiness
 will want to become just like Jesus.
That way they will be close to God.
And God will be close to them.

SOME PARABLES

The friends of Jesus once asked him how they should live
    so as to be pleasing to God.
Jesus didn't say,   'Be simple and unimportant,
                        be honest and generous,
                        and trust people.'
He simply fetched a child out of the crowd and said,
    'That's how.'
He was teaching them by **parable.**

A parable is any action or story
    which says something important in picture-language.
Like any good teacher, Jesus did a lot of his teaching
    in this way.

Many of the parables finish in a rather unexpected
    and surprising way.
That is because Jesus wanted to teach people the good news
    about God, who is surprisingly different
    from what most people expect.

This means that each of the parables is a bit of a riddle.
They never say, 'This is the answer.'
They always say, 'What do *you* think?'

LOST AND FOUND

A shepherd had a hundred sheep to look after.
One of them wandered off and got lost.
So the shepherd left the rest of his sheep on the hillside,
   and went off after the one that was lost.
When he found it, he was delighted.
He brought it home on his shoulders.
Then he called in his friends and neighbours, and said,
   'I've found the sheep I lost.
   Let's have a party!'

A woman had a piece of jewellery with ten precious coins in it.
One of them fell off and got lost.
So she put the light on and swept the room very carefully,
   looking everywhere.
When she found the coin, she was delighted.
She called in her friends and neighbours, and said,
   'I've found the coin I lost.
   Let's have a party!'

(Luke 15:4-9)

God is like that.

A hundred sheep to look after

Pigfood

AN EXTRAORDINARY FATHER

A farmer had two sons.
One day, the younger son said,
  'I wish you were dead,
  so that I could have my share of the farm.'
To everyone's surprise, the father shared out the farm to
  the two of them.

The younger son took his share, packed his things,
  and went abroad.
There he had a wild time, spending all his money.

When it had all gone, and he had nothing more to eat,
  he could only find a job feeding pigs.
He got so hungry, he felt like eating the pigfood himself.
Then he thought,
  'What a fool I am!
  Back home there's plenty of food for everyone.
  I'll go back and tell my father how wrong I've been.
  I can't be his son any more, but I can work for him.'
So he went home.

His father had been waiting for him, he felt so sorry for him.
When he saw him coming, the father astonished the
  neighbours by running through the village to meet him,
  and embracing him.
The son began,
  'Father, I've wronged you.
  I can't be your son any more . . . '
But the father stopped him, and said to the servants,
  'Quick, put some new clothes on him,
  and get a meal ready.
  Tonight, we'll have a party for the whole village!'

(Luke 15:11-23)

God is like that.

You stay there, knocking

NEVER TAKE NO FOR AN ANSWER

Suppose you've got a friend who lives near you.
One day visitors arrive at your house late at night.
So you knock up your friend, and call out,
    'Can you lend me some bread?
    I haven't got a thing to give my guests.'
She calls back, 'Sorry, I can't help you.
    The door's locked and we're all in bed.
    I'm not getting up now.'
You stay there, knocking at the door.
At last, your neighbour gets up,
    and gives you what you want.
Not because she's your friend,
    but because she's fed up with your knocking!

(Luke 11:5-8)

God is like that.

They'll enjoy my party

RUDE GUESTS

A rich man wanted to give a party.
He sent out invitations to lots of people

On the day, he sent his son to tell them
   everything was ready.
But each of them started making excuses:
'I've just bought a farm', said one.
   'I've got to go and inspect it.
   Sorry I can't come.'
'I've just got some new farm equipment', said another.
   'I've got to go and try it out.
   Sorry I can't come.
'I've just got married', said a third one.
   'Sorry I can't come'.

When the rich man heard this, he was very upset,
   and said to his son,
   'Right. Go out this moment,
   and bring in the poor and those in need,
   wherever you can find them.
   I'm sure *they'll* enjoy my party!'

(Luke 14:16-21)

God is like that.

A GENEROUS FARMER

One harvest time, a farmer went into town at 6 in the morning,
  to find workmen to help with the harvest.
They agreed on a fair day's wage, and went off to work.
About 9 the farmer went out again,
  and found men still waiting for a job.
So he told them, 'You can go and work for me too,
  for the same wage.'
At midday he did the same again,
  and again at 3 in the afternoon.

At 5 in the evening he went into town again,
  and there were still men wanting work.
'Why are you hanging about all day doing nothing?'
  he asked.
'Nobody has taken us on', they said.
He told them, 'Well, you can go and work for me too.'

At 6 in the evening, the farmer told his foreman,
  'Pay all the workmen their wages,
  starting with the last ones we took on.'
They came up, and each got a full day's pay.
When those who had worked from 6 in the morning came up,
  they expected to get much more.
But they also got just a full day's pay.
So they began to complain.,
  'Hey, those men who came last only did an hour's work!
  We've sweated all day long,
  and you're treating them just like us!'
The farmer replied, 'Do you think that's unfair?
  You've got the day's wages we agreed on.
  Take it and go.
  Why shouldn't I pay these latecomers the same as you?
  Can't I be generous with my money?'

(Matthew 20:1-15)

God is like that.

THE FARMER WHO WENT ON AND ON

A farmer goes out to sow seeds in his field.
As he goes, some seeds fall on the path.
The birds come and eat them up.
   But the farmer goes on.
Some seeds fall on thin soil, on top of rocks.
They grow quickly, and die quickly,
   because they've got no deep roots.
   But the farmer goes on.
Some seeds fall on soil full of weeds,
   and the weeds choke them.
   But the farmer goes on.
Because most of the seeds fall onto good, deep, clean soil.
There, each seed grows ripe, and produces thirty more.
Sometimes sixty.
Sometimes even a hundred.

Farmers never give up sowing seeds
   simply because some get lost.
They know that what they get from the harvest
   is always more than they sowed.

(Mark 4:3-8)

God is like that.

Barnaby's Picture Library

More than they sowed

A place where they would look after him

THE HATED FOREIGNER

A man was going down a lonely road,
    when he was held up by a gang of bandits.
They beat him up, and left him half dead on the road.
Some time later, a clergyman passed by.
He saw the man, but was afraid that if he helped,
    he might not be able to hold the church service.
So he hurried on.
Later a church worker came by.
He was also afraid, and hurried on.

Last of all, a foreigner came down the road.
He felt so sorry for the man, he knelt down,
    bandaged up his wounds, lifted him onto his horse,
    and took him to a place where they would look after him.
Next day, he gave the man in charge half his week's wages.
'Look after him', he said.
'If it costs more, I'll pay you next time I'm by.'

Jesus said that the only one of the three
    who treated the man as God would treat him,
    was a hated foreigner.

(Luke 10:30-35)

He didn't even dare look up

WHO IS CLOSE TO GOD?

Two men were saying their prayers.
One was a very holy person,
    who went to church every Sunday.
The other was a business man,
    who used to cheat people out of their money.

The holy man stood up at the front and prayed out loud:
    'O God, thank you
    for making me different from other people.
    They are greedy, and cheat, and do wicked things.
    This business man behind me, for example.
    Whereas I go without my meals twice a week.
    And I give a lot of my money to the church.'

The business man stayed at the back of the church.
He didn't even dare look up,
    he was so ashamed of the wrong things he'd done.
He kept banging his chest and saying,
    'O God, be kind to me, and forgive me.'

Jesus said the second man was close to God,
    not the first man.

(Luke 18:10-14)

JESUS TOLD HIS STORIES TO LET US KNOW WHAT GOD IS REALLY LIKE

God is like someone who can't rest until he's found what's lost.

God is like a father who goes on and on forgiving.

God is like someone who can't refuse those who keep asking.

God is like someone who invites all the poor to a party.

God is like a farmer who pays people for work they haven't done.

God is like a farmer who is never put off by failure.

God is like a foreigner who does good deeds even to those who hate him.

God is closest to those who are sorry for the wrong things they've done.

Anyone who behaves in the same way, said Jesus, belongs to the 'Kingdom of God'.